OCT 5 '72
APR 13 '73
JUL 2 '73
NOV 1 '73

NOV 15 '73

GEORGETOWN MAY 8 '74

FRIENDS
OF ACPL

W9-DIG-981

my visit to the
DINOSAURS

my visit to the
DINOSAURS

by ALIKI Pseud.
aliki Brandenberg

Thomas Y. Crowell Company   New York

LET'S-READ-AND-FIND-OUT SCIENCE BOOKS

Editors: *DR. ROMA GANS*, Professor Emeritus of Childhood Education, Teachers College, Columbia University

DR. FRANKLYN M. BRANLEY, Chairman of The American Museum-Hayden Planetarium, consultant on science in elementary education

Air Is All Around You

Animals in Winter

A Baby Starts to Grow

Bees and Beelines

Before You Were a Baby

The Big Dipper

Big Tracks, Little Tracks

Birds at Night

Birds Eat and Eat and Eat

The Bottom of the Sea

The Clean Brook

Down Come the Leaves

A Drop of Blood

Ducks Don't Get Wet

The Emperor Penguins

Find Out by Touching

Fireflies in the Night

Flash, Crash, Rumble, and Roll

Floating and Sinking

Follow Your Nose

Glaciers

Hear Your Heart

High Sounds, Low Sounds

How a Seed Grows

How Many Teeth?

How You Talk

Hummingbirds in the Garden

Icebergs

In the Night

It's Nesting Time

Ladybug, Ladybug, Fly Away Home

The Listening Walk

*Look at Your Eyes**

A Map Is a Picture

The Moon Seems to Change

My Five Senses

My Hands

My Visit to the Dinosaurs

North, South, East, and West

Rain and Hail

Rockets and Satellites

Salt

Sandpipers

Seeds by Wind and Water

Shrimps

Snow Is Falling

Spider Silk

Starfish

*Straight Hair, Curly Hair**

The Sun: Our Nearest Star

The Sunlit Sea

A Tree Is a Plant

Upstairs and Downstairs

Watch Honeybees with Me

What I Like About Toads

What Makes a Shadow?

What Makes Day and Night

*What the Moon Is Like**

Where Does Your Garden Grow?

Where the Brook Begins

Why Frogs Are Wet

The Wonder of Stones

*Your Skin and Mine**

*AVAILABLE IN SPANISH

Copyright © 1969 by Aliki Brandenberg. All rights reserved. Except for use in a review, the reproduction or utilization of this work in any form or by any electronic, mechanical, or other means, now known or hereafter invented, including xerography, photocopying, and recording, and in any information storage and retrieval system is forbidden without the written permission of the publisher. Manufactured in the United States of America. L.C. Card 70-78255

1   2   3   4   5   6   7   8   9   10

CO. SCHOOLS
C736181

my visit to the
DINOSAURS

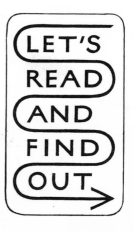

Yesterday I went to see the dinosaurs.
I went with my father and my little sister.
The man showed us where to find the dinosaurs.
He took us up in a big elevator.

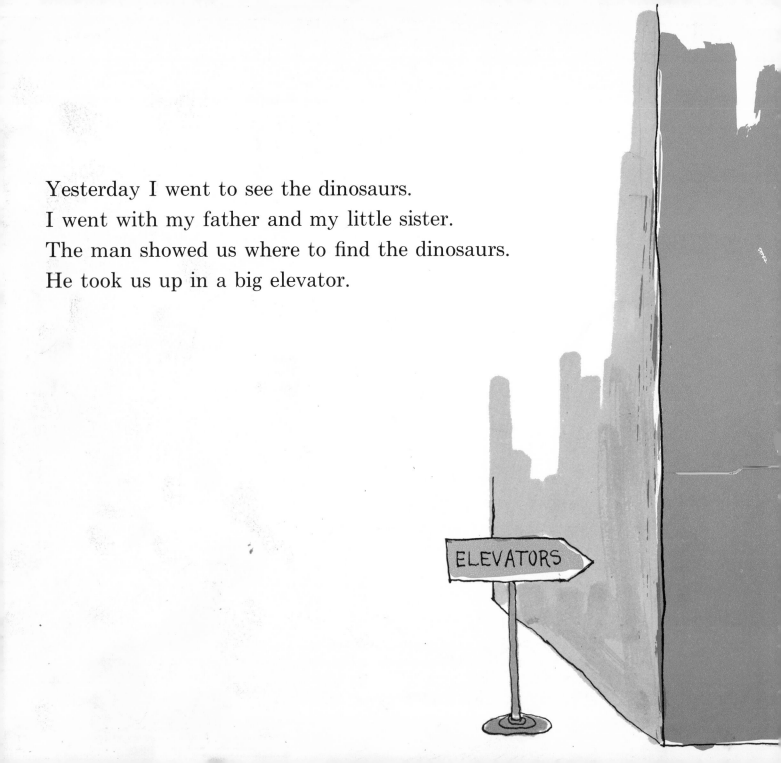

1

We walked down a hall, turned a corner—and there
  they were. Skeletons.
Real dinosaur skeletons.
They were standing in a room bigger than a house.
One skeleton was almost as long as the room.
It looked scary.

My father told my sister and me not to be afraid.
Dinosaurs lived millions of years ago.
No dinosaurs are alive today.

FIRST DINOSAUR HALL

EARLY DINOSAUR HALL

FIRE HOSE INSIDE

QUIET

3

I took a picture of the long dinosaur,
    BRONTOSAURUS.
Then I went over and looked closer.

The skeleton was wired together. Heavy rods held
    it up.
I could see that some of the bones were not real.
They were made of plaster.
What a job it must have been to put this huge
    puzzle together.
How could anyone know where all the pieces fit?

When the dinosaurs died, they were covered with sand and mud. They were buried for millions of years.
The sand and mud turned into rocks, and the dinosaurs' bones became fossils.

In 1822 the first dinosaur fossil was found.
It was found by accident.

After that, many diggers went looking for fossils.
They dug in the rocky earth.

They found fossil bones of dinosaurs.

Some diggers found fossil eggs, which the dinosaurs
had laid in sandy pits.

They even found fossil baby dinosaurs.

It is hard work to take fossils from the ground.
They are often embedded in solid rock.

Paleontologists studied the fossils carefully.
A paleontologist is a scientist who studies animals
and plants of the past.
Paleontologists know when dinosaurs lived and how
dinosaurs lived.
They know what dinosaurs ate.

GORGOSAURUS
MEAT EATER

Some dinosaurs ate meat, and some ate plants.
Giant dinosaurs and duckbill dinosaurs ate plants.
So did horned dinosaurs and armored dinosaurs and plated dinosaurs.
Many of the plant eaters spent most of their lives in the water.

CORYTHOSAURUS
(DUCK BILL DINOSAUR)
PLANT EATER

STYRACOSAURUS
(HORNED DINOSAUR)
PLANT EATER

ANKYLOSAURUS
(ARMORED DINOSAUR)
PLANT EATER

BRONTOSAURUS was a plant eater.

This is the way it looked when it was alive.

Brontosaurus reached down with its long neck in the swamps and ate water plants.

It could lie low and hide from an enemy.

Its eyes were high on its flat head.

It could peek out without being seen.

BRACHIOSAURUS was another giant dinosaur that lived in the water and ate plants.
It was the biggest and heaviest dinosaur there ever was.

15

Another plant eater was TRACHODON, a duckbill.
It had feet that were webbed, like a duck's.
It was a good swimmer.

Trachodon had jaws shaped like a duck's bill.
The jaws were full of teeth.
Trachodon had 1,600 flat teeth to crush and grind
  its food.

PROTOCERATOPS was a horned dinosaur.

ANKYLOSAURUS was an armored dinosaur.

These dinosaurs ate plants, too, but they lived on
land.

They looked so unappetizing that meat-eating dinosaurs left them alone.

Who would want to bite their thick, leathery skin,
covered with bony spikes and plates?

Meat-eating dinosaurs were fast, fierce hunters.

A hungry meat eater like ALLOSAURUS ate any animal it could find.

It was not even afraid to attack Brontosaurus, which was twice its size.

Allosaurus ran on two strong legs.

It caught its prey in its short arms and ripped it apart with big, pointed claws.

Allosaurus ate its food with long, sharp teeth.

My father, my sister, and I went to another hall
  and looked at more skeletons.
There were so many to see that we had to hurry.

HORNED DINOSAUR

DIPLODOCUS was the longest dinosaur. Its body was so big, and its head and mouth so small, that it had to eat its plant food almost without stopping, in order to satisfy its hunger.

This is the way it looked when it was alive.

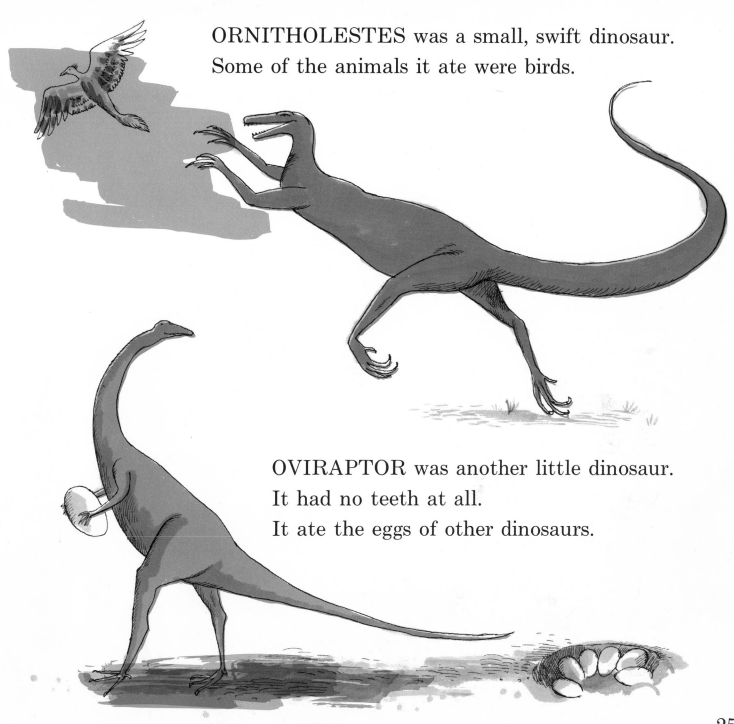

ORNITHOLESTES was a small, swift dinosaur.
Some of the animals it ate were birds.

OVIRAPTOR was another little dinosaur.
It had no teeth at all.
It ate the eggs of other dinosaurs.

We saw a plated dinosaur, fierce-looking
STEGOSAURUS.

It had big, bony plates covering its back, and a
spiked tail to swing at its enemies.

We saw horned dinosaurs, too.
MONOCLONIUS had only one horn.

STYRACOSAURUS had a horn on its nose and a
frill of spikes around its neck.

And TRICERATOPS had three horns on its head—
   one on its nose and one over each eye.
A big, fan-shaped bone protected its neck.
My father said Triceratops could defend itself even
   against TYRANNOSAURUS REX.
I wondered who Tyrannosaurus Rex was.

Then I saw it.

TYRANNOSAURUS REX was king of all the dinosaurs. And the fiercest.

When it walked the earth on its huge hind legs, Tyrannosaurus towered over all the other dinosaurs.

It grabbed them with its small forearms.

It tore them apart with pointed claws and ate them with its long, sharp teeth.

CO. SCHOOLS
C736181

31

I had to stand far away from Tyrannosaurus to take its picture.

My father and my sister looked tiny next to it.

I was glad Tyrannosaurus Rex wasn't alive any more.

When you go to the museum, you will see what I mean.

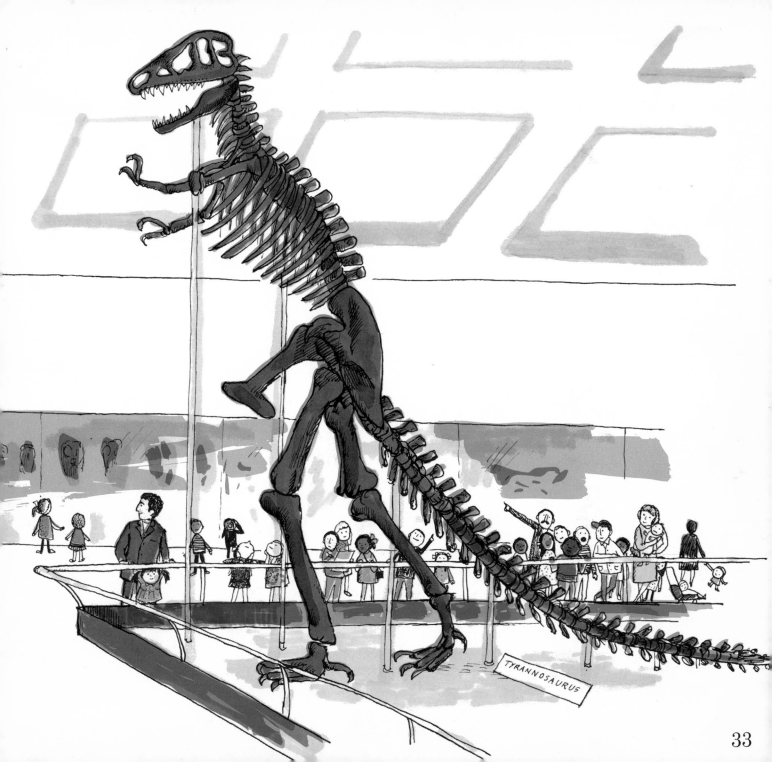

TYRANNOSAURUS

ABOUT THE AUTHOR-ILLUSTRATOR

Aliki worked in many phases of the art field before she began illustrating and writing children's books. Now, when she is not too busy with books, she likes making dolls, puppets, and scenery for the family puppet theater.

Aliki Brandenberg grew up in Philadelphia and graduated from the Museum College of Art. She and her husband, Franz Brandenberg, lived in Switzerland for several years and traveled to many countries.

Now Mr. and Mrs. Brandenberg live in New York City. Their travels take them to many museums with their two young children, Jason and Alexa. It is, in fact, these trips that acquainted the Brandenbergs with the dinosaurs.